ADVICE

written on the back of a business card

*Leaders share their most valued
words of guidance*

Dr. Roger D Smith

/M/

Modelbenders Press

Advice written on the back of a business card: Leaders share their most valued words of guidance.

Modelbenders Press books may be purchased for business and promotional use or for special sales. For information please contact the publisher.

The term *"Advice on the back of a business card"* is a Trademark of Modelbenders LLC.

Visit our web site at www.modelbenders.com

PRINTED IN THE UNITED STATES OF AMERICA

Cover quote *"You can do anything ... but not everything"* was provided by Bill Waite, Aegis Technologies Group.

Designed by Adina Cucicov at Flamingo Designs

The Library of Congress has cataloged the paperback edition as follows:

Smith, Roger
    Advice written on the Back of a Business Card: Leaders share their most valued words of guidance.
    Roger Smith – 1st ed.
    1. Career – Management   2. Businesspeople – Conduct of Life
    3. Business Principles   I. Roger Smith   II. Title

ISBN-13: 978-0-9823040-3-7
ISBN-10: 0-9823040-3-X

Table of Contents

Introduction

What advice would you write on the back of your business card?

Leaders and successful people in every industry and profession are eager and willing to share their advice on success, effectiveness, and moral principles with the generation that is coming after them. They remember all of the mistakes that they made in their careers. They have learned a number of valuable principles that would have been very helpful to them in the early years of their careers.

This book is a collection of over 200 pieces of advice from the people that do the hiring, firing, and promoting in hundreds of organizations. If you want to know what it takes to get ahead or where your priorities should be at work and in life, then you need to read this book carefully and put these words of advice to work.

Each of these leaders was presented with the question:

"Imagine that you are about to give your business card to a young person entering your profession. But first, you turn that card over and write a short piece of advice to help them get started in their career. What would you write on the back of your own business card to help them?"

Their answers are short, quick, and to the point. These are the words that each of them would willingly associate with their name and position by penning it to the back of their own business card. Some leaders chose to quote from famous sources. Some expressed their own unique moral, social, and business principles.

How to Use This Advice

All of this advice is true, useful, and effective ... for different people, at different times, and in different situations. Some of the entries are contradictory, but that does not make any of them less true or less useful. These leaders spent 20, 30, or 40 years learning these lessons in real situations. Some learned by their own trial and error. Some learned from the experience of people who went before them. Some learned from a book just like this one. But all of them offered these as the most important single thing they would share with a young person entering their field.

You can learn many of these lessons yourself by reading this book rather than through your own personal trial and error. But this book is not a novel or a how-to guide. No one can read straight through over 200 unique pieces of advice and say, *"there, I understand all of them and am ready to use them in my life."* You cannot digest the life experiences of 200 people who each have at least 20 years of experience. That is over 4,000 years of human life filled with different challenges, mistakes, and triumphs. After reading 200 of these gems you will remember a few and will find an immediate opportunity to use fewer still.

Introduction

To really benefit from all that this book has to offer you need to consult it many times. As you find yourself in situations calling for help and guidance in each of the areas, you can dip into the advice and find that the words mean much more when you are dealing with a similar challenge.

You can also jump randomly from page to page sampling different ideas and stumbling over some that are meaningful to you right now, but which did not make an impression the first time you read them. This kind of situational meaning is common with all lessons in morals, philosophy, psychology, and theology.

Your goal in buying this book is not to read it completely or to read it quickly. Your goal is to benefit from the advice of experienced people who have been through the same situations that you face. The value you get from applying one idea is much greater than the value of having read all of them quickly.

There are over 200 experienced leaders waiting in the following pages. Each of them offers their best words of advice to you. They are here to make you more successful and effective in your career and your life. Now it is your turn to make the most of this opportunity to learn from them.

Chapter 1

ACTIONS

Bill Waite

Chairman and CTO,
Aegis Technologies Group

"You can do anything... but not everything."

Bill is an incredibly diverse executive and technologist. But even he realizes that people have a limited amount of time and energy. We all have the talent to do anything we want, but none of us has the time and energy to do everything we can think of. Choose your most precious "anything" and do not let the ocean of "everything" overwhelm you.

Brett Christensen

Learning Projects Manager,
Canadian Defence Academy

"Give away everything you know and learn. You will receive tenfold in return."

Brett has learned a lesson that goes back to Biblical times, *"Give, and it will be given to you. A good measure, pressed down, shaken together and running over, shall be poured into your lap."* He knows that you cannot give away your knowledge, help, and expertise without more than that coming right back to help you in return.

Dr. Greg Schow

Senior Program Manager,
Lockheed Martin

"Always volunteer. You have to work anyway, you may as well have some say in what you work on. This gives you a way to control your own destiny."

Many people volunteer for a job before they can be assigned to one. It gives them the opportunity to choose what they will be working on. If the task is recognized as something valuable, then they earn a reputation for stepping forward and for working on important jobs.

Dave Perme

Vice President,
Accenture Defense

"Volunteer for assignments."

The company has a number of jobs that need to get done, by volunteering to do these you show that you are prepared to solve the company's problems, not just your own. Your boss will appreciate and remember this because it is a rare trait. He or she needs many more people who will volunteer for tough jobs.

Dr. Katherine Morse

Senior Staff,
Johns Hopkins University

"Learn to write with precision and clarity. If you can't express your idea, it doesn't exist."

History, society, and technology are built on the works of people who wrote their ideas down. Many more ideas were lost because the creator did not commit them to paper. Years or centuries past before those ideas were rediscovered by someone who made them a permanent part of history by writing them down.

Chapter 1: Actions

Dr. Ricardo Valerdi

Research Scientist,
MIT

"Just because something works in one environment doesn't mean it will work anywhere else."

All sciences, projects, products, teams, organizations, and markets are different—some slightly, some radically. An idea, process, tool, or technique that works one place may not work at all in another. Experience in previous situations is valuable, but it seldom provides a ready made solution for all of today's problems.

Graham Rhodes

Senior Scientist,
Applied Research Associates

"Diversify yourself continuously."

Graham does not believe in absolute specialization. He has lived through enough shifts in business and technology to know that diverse skills are essential if you are going to keep on being valuable to a company and an industry. He believes that diversity of skills is the foundation for a solid future.

Chapter 1: Actions

Dr. Randy Crowe

*Principle Engineer,
Lockheed Martin*

"Stay flexible, don't get a label, and prepare for change."

"When I'm asked by young folks in college about what engineering education to pursue, I've been saying 'become an International Engineer.' This means having a world view and being able to work anywhere, with anyone from any culture. This will be necessary for success. The advice I was given in 1965 was to stay flexible, don't get labeled, and prepare for change. All of that is still true but needs to have the multi-cultural, international emphasis added."

Skip Songy

Chief Scientist,
SPARTA Defense Systems

"Stay flexible in a new position and volunteer to work on and solve your boss' most difficult problems."

Companies hire you for the skills on your resume. But as soon as you start they want you to solve the problems that they have today, and tomorrow, and the day after that. They do not care what you were trained in, they want you to be valuable today by solving today's problems. Be flexible. If you are smart enough to get a good education, then you are smart enough to re-educate yourself on the job.

Tim DiVecchia

*Chief Engineer,
General Dynamics—AIS*

"Focus on breadth of experience before depth!"

Tim is a jack-of-all-trades. He can write software or write business proposals. He can fix computers or fix people problems. He has developed his own talents in a number of areas because those were the areas that his company or project needed at the time. He emphasizes, *"Remember, things change! Be flexible. Adapt!"*

Paul Mauritz

Vice President and General
Manager,
e.magination IG

"Learn how to sell."

"No matter what your profession ends up being, you need to know how to present opportunities and then get backing for them. Whether it is a product, an idea, or an approach. Knowing how to get buy-in will be increasingly important as your career progresses."

Mike Robel

Senior Systems Engineer,
Raytheon

"You have to be a Renaissance
Man."

"It is not enough just to be a good engineer. You have to
have an understanding for how people work, different
ideas and concepts, engineering, and a healthy sense of
skepticism in order to provide a balanced evaluation and
development of a project. I dare say this is how I, a history
major, have been able to turn my wargaming hobby into
the ability to create a variety of simulations."

Roger Smith

CTO,
US Army Simulation, Training, and
Instrumentation

"In the real world there is a difference between being smart and being effective. You get paid to be effective."

No one cares how smart you are if you cannot help the company or the customers deliver a solution. Some people know how to make their intelligence work for them—they are effective. Others wear their intelligence like a badge of honor and look for others to worship them—they have no value.

Chapter 1: Actions

Tiffany Ryan

VP Account Services,
Palio Communications

"Remember that every problem
has a solution just waiting
to be uncovered. Be the one
looking for solutions, not
focusing on the problem!"

We can all see the problem. We are all concerned about the
problem. We all know a hundred ways to stop progress. But
what we really need are people who can find a solution. We
really need people who are not intimidated by the problem,
but are challenged enough to find a solution.

Brett Trantham

*Senior Software Engineer,
Raytheon, Virtual Technologies*

"Seek opportunity in everything you do."

There are connections between everything in the world. The projects, people, companies, knowledge, and experiences that you encounter have oceans of opportunities attached to them. Can you see opportunity in everything you do?

Chapter 1: Actions

Dr. Steve "Flash" Gordon

Manager,
Georgia Tech Research Institute

"Volunteer, stretch, and seek
every logical opportunity to
learn."

"Be the best you can be at what you are doing, and other
opportunities will appear."

Dr. Doug Reece

Research Scientist,
Applied Research Associates

"Always do your best. No matter what the task."

Doug says, "People will remember how good a job you did on the small, simple, unwanted task when the time comes to assign a significant or more desirable job. You may be surprised to find that the original task was more important than you knew."

Chip Brown

Program Manager,
Forterra Systems

"Strive for a commitment to
excellence."

Commit yourself to be excellent—not mediocre, not poor,
not the person with the most excuses or the most sick
days.

Ed Boyd

Account Manager,
Sun Microsystems

"Always be ready for and embrace change."

"This includes change in technology, economics, social status, friendships, enemies, and all aspects of your job. Change is one of the only things in life that is certain. You should make change happen because change is what drives progress. Change makes life interesting."

Chapter 2

ATTITUDE

Marco Pluijm

Manager Port Development,
Amsterdam Port Authority

"If I can't be myself, who else should I be?"

Marco is responsible for the gigantic sea port in Amsterdam, The Netherlands. Even jobs that big can be accomplished by someone who is comfortable being themselves rather than the sterilized "suit" that most companies like to impose on employees. Don't give up being who you really are because you believe that all successful people conform to some sterile standard. They don't.

Chester Kennedy

Vice President of Engineering,
Lockheed Martin Simulation
Training and Support

"Knowledge is power but
attitude is the key that starts
the engine."

Chester says that you have to, *"Differentiate yourself by choosing to have a great attitude. I'd take a 2.5 GPA with a great attitude over three 4.0s with poor attitudes."*

Dr. David Pratt

CTO and Fellow,
SAIC

"A positive attitude goes much further."

No one wants to work with a negative complainer who makes everyone else's life more difficult. A positive attitude will cause people to include you in projects, welcome your advice, and embrace you as part of the team.

Warren Katz

Owner,
MaK Technologies

"Congratulations! You are
about to attempt something
that older, experienced professionals think is impossible,
but your ignorance will
permit you to achieve it."

Optimism and naiveté can be wonderful things. They see past the barriers and failures that stop more experienced people from going further. Young talent does not know what is impossible and they work hard until they have accomplished at least one impossible thing.

Dr. Scott Langhorst

Instructional Systems Specialist,
U.S. Army

"Sometimes opportunities are strangely disguised as disappointments, and many of today's obstacles can become tomorrow's shining achievements."

Remember that your career will take many twists and turns as you engage life. You do not have a crystal ball to show you which events will make a big difference in your future.

Chapter 2: Attitude

Frank Tanke

Manager,
Michelin Fleet Solutions

"Believe in yourself."

It is a pity that so many people are carrying around an inferiority complex that was born and reinforced in high school. Real people in the real world are completely different from high school children. Your education, experience, and internal growth have made you capable and competent. The world will embrace you if you believe in yourself and what you are doing. Stop waiting for someone to break the magic spell of your insecurity—throw it off yourself right now.

Per Gustavsson

Senior Research Scientist,
Saab

"You should always be skeptical of people who give you advice."

Not all advice is intended for your good. Some of it is premeditated to serve the needs of the person giving the advice. Some of it is just wrong. You need to evaluate the advice you get and determine for yourself whether it is good, true, and valuable.

Chapter 2: Attitude

Peter Lutz

Business Systems Consultant,
AIG

"Know yourself and the value
you add from your skills,
attitudes and abilities."

Do you know what you re good at? Do you know where
your skills are? Do you know what really makes you happy?
You need to find out. You need to understand what value
you can add. Do not wait for someone else to tell you.

Dave Guerrero

*Group Manager,
Northrop Grumman Corp.*

"Believe in what you're doing. Stay focused and demand the best of yourself and others."

Create a social environment around you that is focused on being excellent. Do not join or create a clique that is trying to do as little as possible.

Brett Butler

Chief Software Engineer,
SAIC

"Trust your judgment and make sure your views are known."

You cannot remain silent in all meetings and working discussions. If you do not contribute your views and thoughts, then why should you be there? You were not just hired for your working hands and your working mind.

Dave Edstrom

Chief Technologist—Global
Systems Engineering,
Sun Microsystems

"Life is short. Death is certain. If you do not make your own decisions now, time will make them for you."

You have to think for yourself and follow your own advice. You may consider the wisdom of many other people and learn from their experiences, but you cannot be a pawn who is forever carrying out the instructions of someone else.

Ken Shuster

Added Value Solutions

"You cannot read the handwriting on the wall if you are one of the bricks."

This advice comes from Colin Beveridge's Trillion$Bonfire. Ken explains that, "There is a natural tendency to want to be a part of or accepted into the group. When you allow yourself to submit to this tendency then you become part of the wall. You can still read the writing on the wall if you stand aside from or at a distance from those encased within the wall. If you do not buy into the 'good of the organization' concepts and look to the good of the collection of individuals, then you have a hope of being a brick but not mortared into the wall."

Laurent Duperval

President,
Duperval Consulting

"State your opinion even if it goes against the crowd."

"If you feel strongly against an issue, learn to present and argue the facts compellingly. Doing so logically, while appealing to everyone's self-interest as well as the best interests of the company, is an uncommon skill, one that has tremendous value for any corporation."

Chapter 2: Attitude

Rob Coble

Career Development & Industry Outreach,
Full Sail University

"Proceed with equal parts confidence and humility."

Rob says, *"You need to be confident in your ability to get the job done, which means you also need to be humble enough to know that you will need to continue learning in order to achieve your accomplishments."*

Chapter 3

GOALS

Al Morasso

Director,
Educational Testing Service

"Neither the peaks, nor the valleys in your career should concern you, but rather the plateaus."

"It is at the plateau where one can become too comfortable. You can become closed to change, adaptation, and risk. You become a dinosaur and dispensable. There is no security in that."

Mike Daconta

CTO,
Accelerated Information
Management LLC

"Money is a byproduct, focus
instead on making something
great."

Only the U.S. Treasury and counterfeiters spend their time
directly making money. Your efforts cannot get money
directly, you have to make something great that has value
to other people.

Wayne Lindo

Senior Systems Engineer,
DEI Services Inc.

"Dream and visualize where
you want to be in the future—
plan it, and work it."

You cannot achieve your dreams if you do not know what
they are. Take the time and make the effort to extract and
codify your dreams. Then work toward achieving them
every day.

Bill Waite

Chairman and CTO,
Aegis Technologies Group

"Be careful what you wish for..."

Who would wish for hardships, failures, and obstacles? We all want the fruits of success, but without the struggle to earn them. Wealth without wisdom can make your life miserable.

Dr. Ernie Page

Technical Staff,
MITRE Corp.

"Plastics."

Steel. Railroads. Electricity. Automobiles. Computers. Internet. Each of these captures in a single word the idea of looking for opportunity in new technology and new products. Some things have the power to change the world and to enrich the people who get on board.

John Walker

Founding Director,
Navigant Consulting

"Don't target some fantastic final outcome from the get-go. Take your assets, experience, and skills right now and leverage them into the next higher thing."

John explains, "In other words, constantly look for opportunities to sharpen and enhance your brand to the world. I find that if you do that and you are always conscious of your brand in all of the decisions you make, then you position yourself for success."

Marc-Alain Mallet

*Director of Business Development and Research Support,
National Research Council Canada*

"Know from the start whether your goal is a specific career or wealth."

Wealth and a career field are not necessarily mutually exclusive. They both come with challenges and rewards but they often take very different paths.

Dr. Aubrey Lee

Management Consultant,
SESCO

"Look to the long run. Don't sweat the short run. But figure out how to fix it."

You have a long life and career ahead of you. The contribution of that life can be measured in decades but the progress made in one day can be minimal. Keep your eye and your mind on the bigger goals while taking small steps every day.

LtCol. Peter Garretson

Chief,
Air Force Future Science and
Technology Exploration

"Look at the bios of people at the top of your organization to see what they did early in their careers."

Peter knows that an organization promotes people with specific traits and accomplishments. You need to look at those who have gone before you to see what the rewarded traits and accomplishments are where you work. They are not a secret, but most people never look for them.

Chapter 4

HARD WORK

Dr. David Pratt

CTO and Fellow,
SAIC

"Always find a way to make yourself useful."

Your boss will give you assignments and responsibilities. But that is not all there is to do. Look around and find more ways to make a difference, to increase your contribution. Do not rely on your boss to make you valuable to the company. Take that responsibility on yourself.

Heather Stagl

Organizational Transformation Coach,
Enclaria, LLC

"If you see something that should be better, don't wait for someone else to fix it."

You do not need permission for everything that you do. You just need to act on your own initiative. Knowing how to improve something is all the permission you need in most cases. You will go a lot further in life and your career by overstepping the boundaries than by under-stepping them.

Bill Waite

*Chairman and CTO,
Aegis Technologies Group*

"There is no free lunch."

This is an abbreviation of a famous quote from one of Robert Heinlein's novels. No one is going to hand you a golden opportunity. You are going to have to work for it and put in the time to show that you are worth more status, more money, better location, or larger perks. If you want lunch you are going to have to work for it.

John Hathaway

*Software Architect,
Dow Jones*

"Do more than is assigned to you."

John was a software programmer deployed to Iraq during Desert Storm. He learned to work practically non-stop for weeks on end. That habit and that endurance has stayed with him. He can and does accomplish far more than he is officially assigned to do. The limit on the amount of work you do is set by you, not by your boss, not by the assignment.

David Bergerson

Vice President,
Sixpoint Partners

"Just do it...those who wait, lose."

What are you waiting for? Jump in and do what your hand has found to do. You will get a lot farther by starting now than by starting next week.

Ian Rendall

Head of Executive Search, Dynamic Positions

"Never let them see you coming."

Ian believes that you should not announce every move you make and every plan you have. Move forward strongly, but silently. You know your objective and so do the people who need to help you get there. But the whole office does not need to know your plan.

Jorge Cadiz

Manager,
Oasis Advanced Engineering

"Always work hard, and endeavor to do so effectively."

There is no substitute for hard work. Focusing this work on something meaningful is the definition of effectiveness. Make all of your work count by focusing on important tasks and then pour all you have into it.

Meghan DiGregory

Senior Business Systems Analyst,
Palladium

"Innovation, motivation, execution!"

Meghan believes in creating new ideas and products, stirring your inner desire to bring those to market, and then executing the plan to get them there.

Phillip Skiffington

Account Manager,
MI Source

"You get out of this job what you put into it."

"The technology industry is a fast paced environment, if you're not willing to come in every day and hustle from the morning until the evening then it's not for you. Keep hustling and working and as long as you put in the effort the results will come."

Sarah McDaniel

Marketing Director,
Sarah Thomas Roth Skin Care

"Do your homework."

"Know ahead of time who you're going to meet, what you'll be talking about, and find something to contribute to whatever meeting or conversation you'll be a part of."

Lee Barnes

Corporate Lead Executive,
Northrop Grumman

"Do you not know that in a race all the runners run, but only one gets the prize? Run in such a way as to get the prize."—1 Corinthians 9:23-25

Lee interprets this as, *"Apply yourself wholeheartedly."*

Arlene Ellis

Account Executive,
22Clicks

"Discipline—more than talent, ambition, or connections—is the most accurate indicator of future success."

Discipline will allow you to accomplish more in a day than other people accomplish in a week. It will allow you to succeed at tasks much faster than your peers and give you the opportunity to move to more influential positions.

Seth Lytle

Senior Programmer Analyst,
Campus Crusade for Christ
International

"Despite the current trends, hard work over time will still pay off!"

The rewards from society, companies, and organizations are earned through hard work—smart hard work.

Bill Back

Program Manager,
Accenture Inc.

"Determine what special value you can provide that would be difficult to replace."

Though there are many people in your organization, there is some unique contribution that you can make. You have a talent for something that is rare in other people. Try to contribute your unique abilities, rather than mimicking the strengths of other people.

Sean Murphy

Lead Software Engineer,
Alion Science and Technology

"Force yourself out of your comfort zone every once in a while, it could be the most rewarding thing you can do."

Your comfort zone is designed by what you already know how to do. Your comfort zone is "the box" that people are always trying to get out of. If you are scared and uncomfortable, then you are learning and growing outside of the box.

Catherine Wyman

Program Director,
DeVry University

"True happiness comes from service to others."

Your service to others will advance society in some way, create value, bring wealth—and contribute to your personal happiness.

Chapter 5

INTEGRITY

Roger Goff

HPC Architect and Principle Engineer, Sun Microsystems

"Never sacrifice your integrity, it is the one thing you take with you everywhere you go."

Your personal integrity came with you to this job and it will leave with you. You do not leave this behind when you change jobs and you cannot escape any compromises you make in your own integrity.

Chapter 5: Integrity

Rusty Roberts

Lab Director,
Georgia Tech Research Institute

"Be yourself, don't pretend to
be someone else."

You know who you really are. You can choose to be that
person, to contribute that person to the world. Or you can
choose to mimic someone else and contribute a cheap copy
of that person to the world. The world really needs more
unique and original copies of unique and original people.

Oleg Dulin

Senior Software Developer,
Knight Capital Group

"It is easy in the world to live after the world's opinion. It is easy in solitude to live after our own. The great man is he who in the midst of the crowd keeps with the perfect sweetness the independence of solitude."
—Ralph W. Emerson

Emerson was famous as the philosopher and writer living in the woods. He was able to see the essentials of life in solitude and in the crowded city. It is much more difficult to be true to your principles when pressured on all sides by other people.

Chapter 5: Integrity

Johnny Garcia

President,
SIMIS

"Quantity is good but most people do not remember Quantity. Quality trumps Quantity. So when you do something, strive for Quality."

"Quality requires attention to every detail. Quality is the ultimate benchmark no matter what business you are in. I use this piece of advice every day of my professional career and life."

Mark Phillips

Vice President,
MASA Group

"Integrity in life, business, and engineering is everything. Be honest, but respectful even when you know the advice isn't appreciated."

When you have to make tough decisions with tough people in challenging times it can be difficult to maintain your principles. Being honest and doing what is right might be very difficult, but you will always regret compromising your integrity in the pursuit of smaller goals.

Elizabeth May

Business Development Manager,
Cubic Defense Applications

"Integrity First.
Service Before Self.
Excellence In All You Do."

Elizabeth focuses on providing excellent services to her customers. She knows that there are many people competing for the business she is after and only by striving for excellence will she be the one to bring that business to her company. She recommends hard work and integrity over shady dealings.

Dr. Agostino Bruzzone

Director, Modeling and Simulation Institute,

University of Genoa

"Act always with regard to real ethical values."

Agostino believes that, *"Your reputation will be very important for your professional future, but is also among the most valuable personal assets that you possess."*

Dr. Andreas Tolk

Associate Professor,
Old Dominion University

"Your integrity is your most valuable characteristic."

Andreas says, "Better to loose a contract or two than to loose your integrity by working against your beliefs. It will pay off at the end of the day."

Bill Waite

Chairman and CTO,
Aegis Technologies Group

"Shit happens, don't panic, know the truth, and do the right thing."

Don't let difficult situations cause you to panic. Everyone faces difficulty. Just keep doing what is right. The crisis will pass and you will come out stronger and with your integrity intact.

Bruce Schwanda

Defense Industry Consultant

"Be honest with your clients as well as with yourself."

Do not lie to yourself and do not lie to your clients. You need them and they need you. Work on a long term, supportive, and honest relationship.

Gabriel Ruiz

Army Program Field Executive,
CDW-G

"Do what's right, even when no one is watching."

There are times when you can be dishonest and no one will know. No one but yourself. Do you want to live with someone whose integrity is really just a show for the outside world?

Chapter 5: Integrity

Jorge Cadiz

Manager,
Oasis Advanced Engineering

"Above all else, maintain your
integrity."

Keep your integrity at the top of your list of priorities.

Leaders share their most valued words of guidance

Kelly Pounds

Vice President,
i.d.e.a.s. Learning

"Be responsible and never ever lie."

Shoulder the tasks that belong to you, deliver on your promises, and be honest with those around you.

Chapter 5: Integrity

Octavio Ballesta

Business Unit Leader,
DBAccess

"You do not need to look else-
where to find answers if you
are faithful to your core values,
your guiding principles, and
your professional ethics."

You came to this job with your core values and principles.
You do not need someone else to tell you what is right and
wrong. Let your own values guide your actions.

Ron LaPedis

Principle,
Seacliff Partners International

"To thine own self be true."
William Shakespeare

Ron insists that, "I would rather leave a job than suffer for it ethically, morally, or by sacrificing happiness."

Steve Detro

Director of Business Development,
L-3 Link Simulation & Training

"Maintain your personal integrity, first and always."

Steve is part of a very tightly connected professional community. He realizes the importance of integrity in an environment where your actions will be known by almost everyone.

Tim Murphy

Owner,
Perkins & Murphy

"Always do the right thing for your clients, no matter what. Check yourself on this constantly."

Are you working for the good of your clients, or just your own good? Always make sure that you do not compromise your clients' interests in an effort to bring all of the benefits to your side of the table.

Dr. Tony Valle

Chief Scientist,
SPARTA Inc.

"Remember that in the long run, you will succeed if you remain honest, diligent, and loyal. Politics and playing games are for suckers."

Playing office politics is a big distraction from really doing the work that is valuable to the organization. You cannot spend your time playing the game and still get valuable work done. How can an organization survive if no one is working because they are playing the political game?

Wes Woodruff

Business Development,
EDS

"Be true to yourself, your goals, your ideals, and your ethics."

You are a unique person with unique plans and unique contributions to be made in the world. Be true to this uniqueness. Do not become a copy of someone else.

Dr. Dylan Schmorrow

Assistant Director for Human Systems,

Office of the Secretary of Defense

"Schmorrow Rule #1: Never Lie to Yourself."

Dylan explains, "This means you must understand your weakness and know in your heart that you are likely not the smartest, nor the hardest working person on the planet. While you must be extremely confident to succeed, you must also know yourself better than anyone and employ your talents accordingly. If you can be honest with yourself about the uniqueness of you, then you are more than halfway to success."

Rick Davenport

Senior Systems Engineer,
MC Dean, Inc.

"Develop and protect your reputation as a truthful person."

You must work to create a reputation for being truthful. But you must also work to protect it. Do not let misunderstandings or outright lies damage your reputation.

Dr. Jeff Wilkinson

Chief Scientist & CTO,
MYMIC

"Be ethical—not just legal.
Your reputation transcends
your paycheck."

Jeff believes that, "The tough reality is that following this advice is rarely going to provide a fast track to the top. In fact, in some circles, this can be a barrier to success."

Leo Holly

Lead Systems Engineer,
MITRE

"If you find yourself being asked to do things that are questionable or unethical, change departments or even companies."

Leo believes that, "You may not make as much money, but you'll be able to sleep at night and never have to worry about being on the wrong end of a civil or criminal investigation. The older you get, the more your peace of mind is worth."

Craig Fones

Defense M&S Account Manager,
ESRI

"Never underestimate the value of trust and integrity."

Craig says, "If you are honest and make ethical decisions, you will never find yourself in a position of having to apologize or explain your actions."

Michael Freeman

Manager,
Camber Corp.

"Be honest and never lie."

Mike says, "While telling the truth can be difficult up front, it's much easier in the long run."

Chapter 6

LEADERSHIP

LtCol. Peter Garretson

Chief,
Air Force Future Science and
Technology Exploration

"Duty is knowing what needs
to be done and when it needs
to be done without having to be
told that it needs to be done."

What is your duty in life, at work, and with family? Do you
know your responsibilities? Are you carrying them out?

Chapter 6: Leadership

Jim Stogsdill

CTO, Mission Systems, Accenture

"Follow the rules, until you're ready not to."

Rules and morals are two different things. The rules were made by other people in other times. What does it take to make things work here and now? Don't let the rules stop you from solving problems and being effective. You are guided by your higher morals, not by the lower rule book.

Catherine Wyman

Program Director,
DeVry University

"Show up no matter what."

Be dependable. People need you and your skills. Are you going to be there when the work needs to get done? Or do you have hundreds of excuses why you are not able to serve?

Sandy Veautour

Chief Systems Engineer,
U.S. Army Simulation and
Training

"Observe everyone where you work. Emulate what the superstars do. Notice what the not so successful people do—and don't do that."

The superstars did not get where they are by working in secret. Their behaviors are out in the open for anyone to observe and emulate. Or you can emulate the losers. Which will you choose?

Andrew Jamison

CEO,
Scalable Display Technologies

"Follow the money."

If you are trying to make a successful company, go where the money is. Rich problems are not necessarily harder than poor problems, they are just the problems that people are willing to pay to have solved. Don't waste your time solving problems that no one is interested in.

Sandy Kearney

Global Director of Government
Research Initiatives,
IBM, T.J. Watson Research Center

"Be a Doer!"

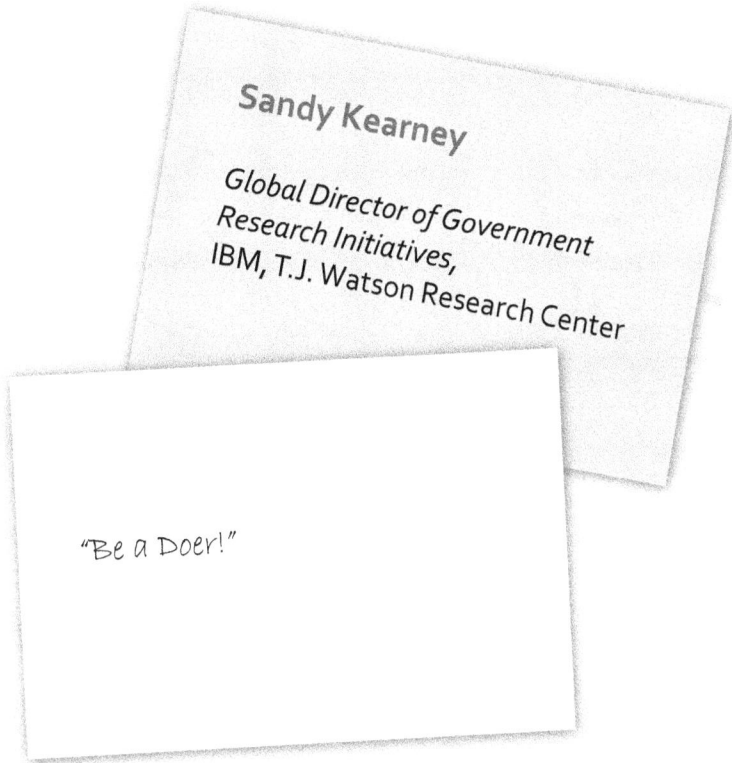

Sandy says, *"There are three types of professionals: Think-
ers, Talkers and Doers."* You should be a doer.

Andy Smith

Owner,
Halldale Media

"If you feel someone in your company is holding your business back, however close to you they maybe, deal with the problem as professionally and rapidly as you can."

Incredibly practical. Dealing with problem people is one of he hardest issues that leaders face. We all avoid confrontation even when it can ruin the business.

Dr. Margaret Loper

Chief Scientist,
Information Technology &
Telecommunications Laboratory,
Georgia Tech Research Institute

"Leadership is not about being the smartest person on the team, it's about knowing how to bring together the best talent to solve a problem."

When you enter a new field you really want to be the smartest person who is solving the problems. But over time you learn that there is a lot of unused potential in the organization because most people do not know how to tap it. Leaders work on tapping the potential of ten or twenty people, rather than trying to do the work of two or three themselves. No matter how smart you are, you cannot do the work of an entire team yourself.

Leaders share their most valued words of guidance

Patrick Samama

President & CEO,
MASA Group

"Don't look for a job, look for a leader."

Patrick says that when you are interviewing, *"Make sure that you meet with all the people you are going to work with, and assess whether they can help you grow on your first job. You will rapidly discover whether you will be able to learn from your future boss by talking to those who work for him or her."*

Rod Olson

Principle Business Development Manager, Rockwell Collins

"Preparation yields confidence, confidence yields credibility, and credibility yields leadership."

If you want to become a leader, there are definite paths to that kind of position. Preparation, confidence, and credibility are a great start.

Brian McNeill

Senior Team Lead,
International Monetary Fund

"Always step forward and quickly accept responsibility for your own mistakes."

Brian says, "You will find that many of your colleagues will dissemble and rationalize when confronted with a difficult situation. But, someone who points out an error by saying, 'I'm sorry. I made a mistake. Here's what I think we should do to fix it' will be remembered - especially by his or her peers and subordinates."

Dr. David Pratt

CTO and Fellow, SAIC

"I'm not your friend, I'm your boss."

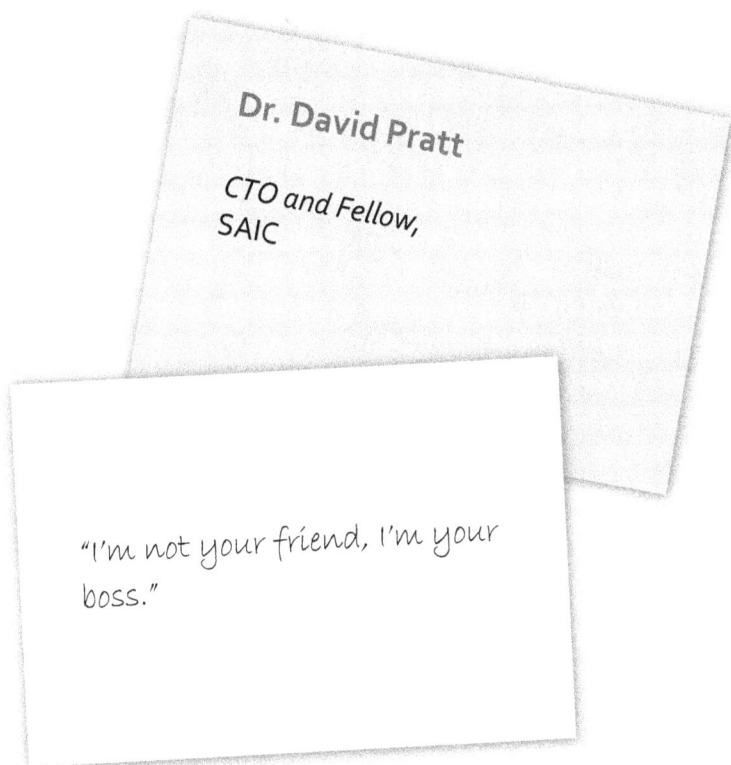

Too many young people come into a business assuming that everyone is in the same chummy club of friends. But it is still true that the boss gives guidance and has a bigger purpose than being your friend or being liked. A good boss is there to make people more effective in achieving a corporate project. If that means cracking heads and making enemies, then that is what he will do.

Donald A. Philpitt

Deputy Director,
Joint Coalition Simulation
Systems (JCSS)

"While every tree in the forest is important, sometimes one must be focused more on the health of the forest than on the health of an individual tree."

When hard times come to a business, people sometimes lose their jobs. It is not always a statement of problems with the person, but more of problems in the organization. Trimming the staff is an effort to save the entire company, not a judgment on specific individuals. When this happens to you move on with your head high and your confidence intact.

Muriel Rukeyser

American Poet

"I am in the world to change the world."

You are here to make a difference—not to fit in, not to be status quo, not to smooth the waters. Make a difference. Make waves. Make change happen.

Randy Shumaker

Director,
Institute for Simulation and Training,
University of Central Florida

"Seize opportunity; don't wait until you are sure you are ready."

When change creates new opportunities, the people who seize it are working from their confidence and enthusiasm, not from any special prior experience. They are attracted by the challenge and the rewards, not by formal preparation because that does not exist yet.

Chapter 7

LEARNING

John Hathaway

Software Architect,
Dow Jones

"Constantly ask yourself: Can this organization do without me? If the answer is 'Yes', then work on changing this to 'Absolutely Not'."

Are you essential or are you optional? Can you answer this question honestly? Or do you need some mentors to help you see it clearly? If you are optional, you can and must do something about that. The people who are essential did not get that way without working at it.

Matt Kraus

VP and Principle Scientist,
Applied Research Associates

"Periodically work in different areas to create a broad background—but ultimately specialize in a single area."

Work and experience broadly. The world is incredibly diverse. You need to let yourself see and experience many different things before you focus on your specialty. Trying many different jobs in your teens and twenties is a great way to discover what you are really interested in.

Al Morasso

Director,
Educational Testing Service

"Take ownership of and personal responsibility for your own career by investing in yourself. If you don't or won't, then why should anyone else?"

Who is most responsible for your career? Who is investing the most in you? The answer to both questions had better be, "me". You do not have a Fairy Godmother out there who will take care of your life and make your dreams come true. Your dreams are your responsibility. Get to work on them now.

Chapter 7: Learning

Albert Johnson

Member, Board of Directors,
Industrial Research Institute

"Understand yourself."

For too many people the phrase, *"You don't know Jack"* is an indightment against knowing themselves (they are Jack). If you don't know yourself, then how can you be responsible for guiding your own life? You need to know all about Jack.

Nephi Lewis

Product Manager,
Rockwell Collins Simulation and
Training Solutions

"Be not deceived with the first appearance of things, for show is not substance."—English Proverb

To really understand a situation at work you need to think about what happened, who the players were, and what history is involved. An event is seldom isolated and self evident in its meaning.

Dr. Ben Amaba

Executive,
IBM

"Create a board of directors
to advise you and guide you
through your professional
career."

Ben says, "Choose people you trust and hold in high regard
for the same principles you espouse. Keep your board fresh
and up to date on your goals and strategy. Elicit feed-
back periodically and balance their input." You may call
it a board of directors advisors, or mentors—but identify
people who can give you guidance on the direction of your
career. It will save you a lot of personal trial and error.

Dave Perme

Vice President,
Accenture Defense

"Find out for yourself. You will gain the knowledge and expertise, and people will seek you out."

Learn to do things yourself. Dig into the project, product, or organization and learn more about it than everyone else knows. Most people just skate around on the surface of this knowledge, never understanding its depths.

Graham Rhodes

Senior Scientist,
Applied Research Associates

"Continuously study a wide variety of topics, both within your discipline and far beyond."

Graham has a Renaissance mind, "If you are a programmer, spend a lot of time in the arts—painting, photography, animation, music, creative writing—at least one or two evenings a week. If you're an artist, learn to do some programming. If you're an engineer, don't believe the old school engineering approaches will last forever. Study the new ways."

John Hathaway

Software Architect,
Dow Jones

"Stay current with technology."

Technology moves like lightning and we are all challenged to keep up with the changes. But falling behind is not an option. If you want to work in a technology field you will be updating your skills for your entire career.

Ken Shuster

Added Value Solutions

"The words of others are not important, what they mean is."

Do you hear what other people are saying? Do you know why they are saying it and what it means? Listen. Listen. Listen. You have two ears and one mouth. Try listening twice as much as you talk.

Dr. Margaret Loper

Chief Scientist,
Information Technology &
Telecommunications Laboratory,
Georgia Tech Research Institute

"Don't be afraid to ask questions—it is not a sign of weakness."

Inquisitiveness is a sign of greatness. It is a trait of Nobel prize winners, geniuses, and the people who really make a difference in the world. Asking questions is the quickest path to new knowledge. Richard Feynman, the Nobel Physicist, used to say that "People think I am slow because I ask a lot of these dumb questions." If it is not beneath Feynman, it is not beneath anyone.

Chapter 7: Learning

Rusty Roberts

*Lab Director,
Georgia Tech Research Institute*

*"Ask questions, learn
something new everyday!"*

Can you imagine how well educated you will be if you learn something new every day? How many days pass for the average person before they learn one new thing? You can learn twice as much easily, three times as much with minimal effort, and four times as much just by being curious. Children used to be challenged to read the dictionary or a set of encyclopedias. You have Wikipedia and the entire Internet.

Troy Crites

Sector President,
SPARTA

"Do your Homework."

Troy says, "In other words be more prepared than everyone else in the meeting, and always know the 'Why' behind your computer generated results."

Dave Kirks

Vice President,
Bank of America

"Learn the business value of
projects you manage."

Every project is not of equal value in an organization. Some
are essential to its survival. Some are incidental. Others are
a drag on the mission of the organization. You want to be
working on projects that are essential for survival. You cannot be indispensible if your project is not indispensible.

Amit Dey

Director of IT,
MELT Services

"3 things to NEVER do...
1) NEVER say 'it can't be done'
2) NEVER stop learning
3) NEVER give up."

Amit says, "The company I was working with shut its doors after 13 years and I was forced to find other work to replace my 'expected' income. All three of these rules have helped me rise through the technology ranks over time and keep moving forward. Most recently, these 3 rules helped me obtain a new position in less than 3 days after the doors closed at my old company."

Jami Carroll

President & CEO,
Prisidien Security Solutions

"Balance your formal education with real world experience. Rotate that experience with different organizations to get different perspectives and find a mentor to help you progress along the path."

In the real world, nothing works the ways it is explained in the textbook. The real world is too messy and complicated to be explained in school and to be understood by people who have not lived it yet. Your education is a great start, but it is far from all that you will need to know to be effective on the job. If you can find a mentor who will guide you, you will learn and progress much further than if you do it alone.

Shawn Lindsey

Director of Government Services,
TEKsystems

"Become a problem solver and consummate learner. Align with mentors. Positive optimistic attitudes are contagious."

Shawn's advice is like a casserole, lots of ingredients mixed together. The purpose of constant learning is to be able to solve problems. Knowledge for its own sake can be very comforting and internally rewarding. But you do not get external rewards until you apply your knowledge to a problem that is meaningful to others. A mentor can be very helpful in guiding you toward problems that need solving and the kind of knowledge you will need to solve them.

Andy Mohler

Department Head,
Northrop Grumman

"Find opportunity in chaos."

In the modern world, chaos shows its head in technology, society, the economy, relationships, organizations, and market changes All of these present problems and opportunities. Chaos and change can destroy your work, or they can give you the opening you need to create something entirely new.

Leaders share their most valued words of guidance

John Mann

Division Manager,
Applied Research Associates

"Study the lives of successful people that have gone before you."

John goes on to say, *"Learn from their mistakes and best practices either through mentoring or reading about their experiences."*

Chapter 7: Learning

Adie Wetzels

Consultant,
YER

"Don't learn from people who want to be an expert, instead you should only learn from the absolute best in the business."

Many well meaning people provide advice and guidance, but without the experience and wisdom to give good advice.

Brett Trantham

*Senior Software Engineer,
Raytheon, Virtual Technologies*

"Be willing to learn from those around you and offer your opinion."

Brett believes that, "Both sides can gain a fresh perspective and learning shows that you're interested in solving the problem."

Chapter 7: Learning

David King

Account Manager,
ImageWear by Walman

"Don't make assumptions."

Assuming you know why something happened is always dangerous. There is an old saying, "to 'assume' is to make an ass of you and me".

Greg Cramer

Manager,
Dunn & Associates

"You know nothing."

Putting it very bluntly, Greg points out that you are just getting started in business and life. You have a lot to learn, just as those who came before you did. Seek out knowledge and wisdom from those around you.

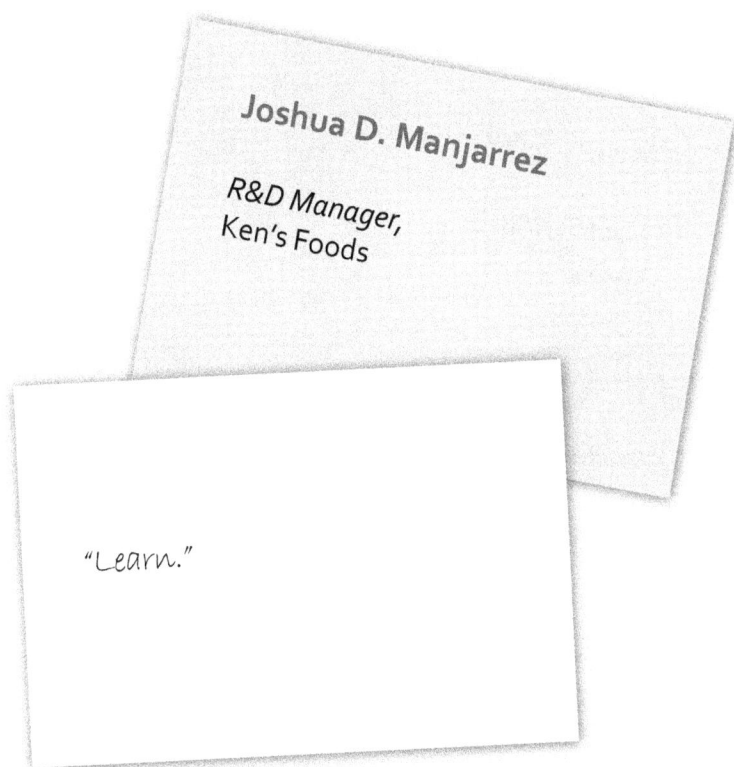

Joshua D. Manjarrez

R&D Manager,
Ken's Foods

"Learn."

Simply put—learn. Do so by experimentation, experience, reading, listening, thinking. But always keep learning.

Mike O'Dell

Chief Scientist,
UUNET

"If you are not afraid, you simply do not understand."

Though Mike helped to build the Internet he was well aware of the huge task he was undertaking and the thousands of dangers and mistakes that lay ahead. It is ok to be afraid. But it is not ok to give up or stop trying.

Chapter 7: Learning

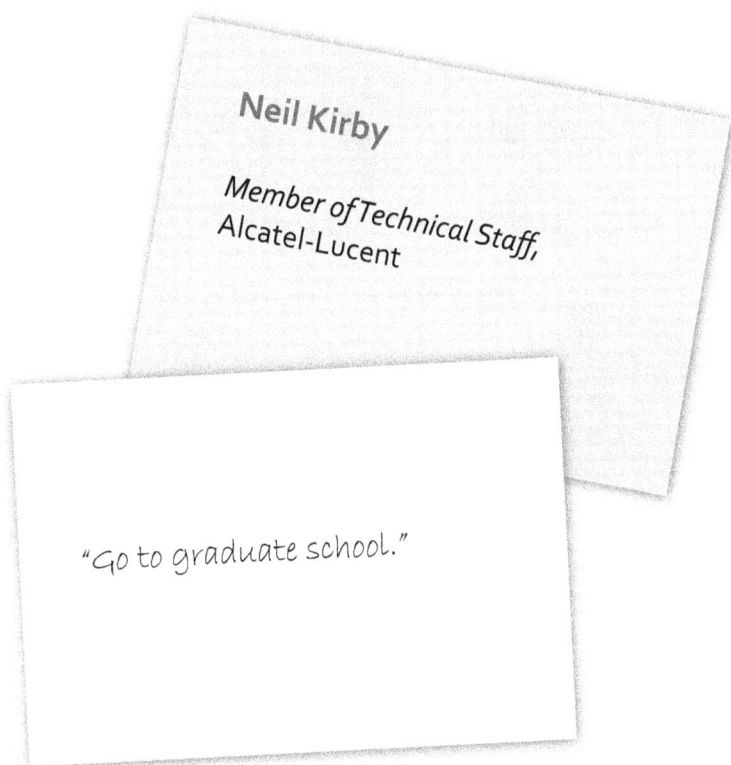

Neil Kirby

Member of Technical Staff,
Alcatel-Lucent

"Go to graduate school."

Neil's career was only possible through advanced education. He understands the power and the value of going beyond a bachelor's degree. He strongly recommends that people continue their formal education through at least a master's degree.

Nephi Lewis

Product Manager,
Rockwell Collins Simulation and
Training Solutions

"Beware of the man of one book."—Latin Proverb

One book represents one idea. This man has no room for many ideas and many perspectives. He has accepted the one idea that he will use and he expects everyone else to accept that idea as well. Though there are millions of other ideas in the world, to this man, they are all wrong and should be abandoned.

Chapter 7: Learning

Richard Boyd

*Chief Architect, Virtual World Labs,
Lockheed Martin Simulation*

"Read 'The Innovator's
Dilemma' by Clayton
Christiansen
Read 'The Singularity is
Near' by Ray Kurzweil
Read 'Engines of Creation' by
Eric Drexler."

Richard has been creating new computer games for almost
two decades. He understands the need to know where the
future lies. He identifies three great books that have helped
him prepare for the future.

"

David Grow

Assistant Program Manager for Instrumentation, Targets, and Threat Simulations,
U.S. Army

"The presence of red ink on your document is an indication that someone cared enough to help you."

David says, "Always remember that a person given a paper with your work on it is trying to add value to what you have done. The presence of red ink on your document is an indication that someone cared enough to help you, and not a criticism of your personal efforts. Your harshest critics are, in truth, your greatest supporters. Treasure them. They will help you go far."

Randy Clarke

Senior Partner & CTO,
Cyberspace Solutions LLC

"Always be willing to expand
your knowledge base. If you
don't continue to explore new
ways to grow you will become
a dinosaur."

You are not a static animal. You are different today from yesterday, and will be different again tomorrow. You are a learning, growing, changing animal. You prosper according to your ability to grow and adapt to changes.

Lou Ford

Project Engineer,
SAIC

"Never stop learning."

In the 21st century there is no point at which you have learned everything you will need to know for the rest of your life—or even everything you need to know tomorrow. We are in the learning century.

Dr. Jeff Wilkinson

Chief Scientist & CTO,
MYMIC

"Read Books. Knowing about the next great thing is not nearly as important as knowing how to really exploit it."

Jeff admits, "I've stolen this from Tim Sander's Book: Love is the Killer App."

Charlie Finan

Chief Architect,
DEG Architecture and Planning,
Intel Corp.

"Be open to new areas."

Charlie says, "Find an emerging technology and explore how it can become the next big thing. Also, respect your peers. They can help you achieve your goals if they respect you."

Dr. Daniel Lacks

Senior Systems Engineer,
Raytheon

"Learning is a continuous activity; it doesn't stop when you graduate. Get to know senior staff and learn from their experiences."

Danny knows that college prepared him to begin learning more practical knowledge from the people who have been doing it for years. The senior staff in your company usually know more than your college professors did. It is time to learn from them.

Dave Neilsen

Founder,
Platform D

"Get paid to learn."

Dave advises, "Don't take a free job for the experience. And don't take a paid job without experience. Instead, find a job that pays and gives you experience, even if it's a hard-working, entry-level job. Finding a paid-to-learn-job isn't easy and usually requires hard work. But nothing worthwhile is easy."

Dr. Amy Henninger

Associate Director,
Office of the Secretary of Defense
for Acquisition, Training, and
Logistics

"What you learned in
engineering school is
necessary but not sufficient.
Most decisions are emotional
and then justified ex post facto.
You'll need more than logic
and facts."

Mature scientists like Dr. Henninger learn that being effective in real organizations requires much more than logic. People are filled with emotions about what they are doing. You need to recognize and work with all of those feelings while applying the data you have so meticulously collected.

Chapter 8

LISTENING

Ken Shuster

Added Value Solutions

"When talking with people—don't."

Most people want to hear their ideas expressed—preferably by themselves. Let them do it.

Chapter 8: Listening

Daryl Mair

Major Account Manager,
SGI

"Listen intently to what others are saying, then act on the wisdom you obtain from it."

One of Stephen Covey's "7 Habits" is, *"Seek first to under-stand, then to be understood."* Listen to what others are saying. Listen intently so that you get the meaning they are putting into the words. Understand why they are expressing these ideas to you. Then you can act wisely.

Gabriel Ruiz

Army Program Field Executive,
CDW-G

"On your first meeting, do 20% of the talking and 80% of the listening."

Listen. The world is trying to tell you everything that you need to know.

Rita Ashley

President,
Job Search Debugged

"Listen. Nothing improves or establishes relationships better than listening... just ask your spouse or partner."

Listening is a big part of building a relationship... with a partner, with a spouse, with a friend, with a customer, and with a colleague.

Susan Shwartz

Manager,
Oppenheimer & Co.

"Let the interviewer finish the question."

During an interview let the interviewer talk. They will often tell you the answer to the question they are asking. Some interviewers are really interviewing themselves. If you encourage them they will conclude that you are brilliant even if you do not say anything.

Rod Olson

Principle Business Development Manager,
Rockwell Collins

"... always be willing to listen ... ask questions ... communicate ..."

You have been dropped into a very rich pool of knowledge, experience, and expertise. Take advantage of that. Ask questions and dig into the unique knowledge that is all around you.

Albert Johnson

Member, Board of Directors,
Industrial Research Institute

"If you listen and understand
well you will always have a
say."

Listen. Understand. Then be heard. Do not attempt to be
heard, heeded, or respected until you have first listened and
understood.

Chapter 9

MORALS

Ken Shuster

Added Value Solutions

"If you don't like what you see in the mirror of your soul—Cleanse, Revive, Recreate."

You are not a finished product cast in stone. You and your life are like a river—constantly moving, changing, and adapting. If you do not like what you have become, then become something different. Keep flowing until you find the place where you belong.

Dr. Aubrey Lee

Management Consultant,
SESCO

"If you think it's not fair, it's not."

Did you think the world was going to be a fair place? It is not. It can be unfair to your advantage, or unfair to your disadvantage. You need to get into a position where the world is working for your advantage.

Troy Crites

Sector President,
SPARTA

"Practice humility at all times."

As effective and important as you might be in the world, there are many people and situations that can bring your world crashing down. You need to practice being humble and recognize that you are a small part of a much bigger picture.

Lee Barnes

Corporate Lead Executive,
Northrop Grumman

"I have seen something else under the sun: The race is not to the swift or the battle to the strong, nor does food come to the wise or wealth to the brilliant or favor to the learned; but time and chance happen to them all."
—Ecclesiastes 9:10-12 "

In spite of all of your wise choices and good habits, there is an element of change at work in the world. Sometimes your work falls apart in spite of your best efforts. This is not an excuse for mediocrity or fatalism. It just helps you prepare for the random effects of a complex and uncontrollable world.

Tim Schmidt

CTO,
US Department of Transportation

"... a career is finite, but family is forever..."

Tim rose to a significant position in government without compromising his relationships with his family. He realizes that his family will be with him long after he puts this job behind him and his influence in the world will carry on through his children for another generation.

Phillip Skiffington

Account Manager,
MISource

"Humble as a beggar, proud as a king."

You may be extremely proud of your contributions and your accomplishments. But remain humble in learning from others and recognizing how much more can be done.

Chapter 10

NETWORKING

Irantzu Gonzalez

International Marketing Manager,
BMW Group

"If you are not online, you do not exist."

In the digital world you cannot survive by just occupying physical space. You have to occupy digital space as well. Your presence online is as real and powerful as your presence in person.

Chapter 10: Networking

Bob Neches

Director, Distributed Scalable Systems Division,
University of Southern California,
Information Sciences Institute

"Don't throw away this card."

Bob explains that he is not saying that knowing him personally is the key to success. But you never know which contacts and relationships are really going to be helpful in our future. Treat each connection as something valuable.

Albert Johnson

*Member, Board of Directors,
Industrial Research Institute*

"Each time you meet a new person, make a game of learning their name and getting their contact information."

Studies show that advances in your career come from your remote network, not your close associates. It is the people you remotely know who are the source of most new opportunities.

Brian Forbes

Director of Engineering,
Intel Corp

"Network outside of your business unit and establish a core group of advisors that have strengths far different from your own."

Brian says, "This has served me well over the years and is probably one of the biggest reasons for my continued success at Intel."

David Bergerson

Vice President,
Sixpoint Partners

"Network religiously with other people's best interests in mind... doing the right thing generates far greater reward."

A network of contacts is not self-centered. It needs to be others-centered. What can you do to help others with their problems? Acting on that will create bonds of trust and gratitude.

Guy Hagens

Owner & President,
Innovation Insight Inc.

"No matter where you are, build the biggest network of people with the most diverse areas of expertise."

Your network should extend far beyond your own company or your specific profession. The world is a rich place with many unusual connections and dependencies. You will need to reach outside of your daily circle for some important changes.

Dr. James Korris

President,
Creative Technologies Inc.

"Manage your contacts scrupulously. Handle your follow-ups meticulously."

Receiving someone's business card is just the first step. You must refresh and develop that connection to keep it active and alive.

Pat Mehan

The Mehan Group,
author "Career of a Lifetime"

"Network today and everyday for the rest of your life—with a sense of giving."

You will get out of your network in proportion to what you put into it. Your contributions will multiply many fold. But there is nothing to multiply if you are putting nothing in.

Leaders share their most valued words of guidance

Richard Baldwin

Program Manager,
Accenture

"Surround yourself with good people."

Rich and I have been friends and professional colleagues for over ten years. He believes that you must, *"Build and nurture a network of trusted professionals that you maintain for a lifetime. Much of your success will depend on others."*

Curtis Conkey

Senior Engineer,
Naval Air Warfare Command

"Network, network, network."

Curtis says, "Do not get locked into narrowly doing 'your job'. Network with others, understand what they are doing, find the correlations to your work, volunteer for tasks outside your job, join professional and social networks, learn the big picture and how you fit into it."

Chapter 11

PASSION

Chris Melissinos

Chief Evangelist and Chief
Gaming Officer,
Sun Microsystems, Inc.

"You must pursue your passion in life. If not, you may fill your wallet but empty your soul."

Chris speaks from experience. He is extremely passionate about his role evangelizing Sun products and it shows in his behavior with customers. An empty soul becomes more painful every year that you continue to move in the wrong direction. Pay attention when you feel the first pangs of a dying soul, it will only get worse.

Grant Marshall

*Investment Advisor,
New England Securities*

"If you don't genuinely believe in the work you do then neither will anyone else."

Faith in your work is contagious. Your customers and coworkers catch it from you—but only if you genuinely have it.

David Bergerson

Vice President,
Sixpoint Partners

"Do something you love... otherwise you will simply work to live."

Why are you here on the Earth? Did you arrive just to serve as fodder for others people's goals and ambitions? Or do you have your own internal purpose and goals? The job you work at should be part of accomplishing your own goals, not just those of the organization.

Chapter 11: Passion

Per Gustavsson

*Senior Research Scientist,
Saab*

"Build Your Talent, Find Your
Arena, Follow Your Passion
and most of all Enjoy Life,
because its more fun that way
and finally ... ; -)"

Build, find, and follow. You are in control of where you work and what you do. Build toward something you love. Find the place where you can do it. Stick to something you are passionate about. And smile because you are living a blessed life.

Leaders share their most valued words of guidance

Peter Lutz

Business Systems Consultant,
AIG

"Be passionate about your work and do your best at everything you do."

People who are successful know that pouring themselves into something they love is much more rewarding and fulfilling that doing the job half-heartedly. We all become proud of the results we achieve when we work hard, rather than being embarrassed at how little our contribution means when we sit back and take it easy.

Ramesh Kumar

CTO,
Eduquity

"Realize your potential!"

Your actions. Your decisions. Your personal efforts are going to determine whether you achieve your purpose here on Earth. You are the deciding factor in realizing your potential.

Chris Giordano

Director of International
Business,
DiSTI Corp.

"Do what you enjoy for a career, the money will come later."

"I am living proof of this one. I started out as a stock broker so I could get rich quick. But I was miserable in my job and it trickled over into my life. I went back to school to do what I enjoyed doing as a hobby—software engineering. After 10 years of helping a young company grow to the global corporation that it is today, I am the software executive I always wanted to be. I am in charge of business all over the world and am making a difference with my input. I enjoy my job and the people I work with. It shines through to everything I do outside of work as well, making my life and the lives of those around me much more fun, stable, steady and exciting."

Mark Friedman

Advanced Concepts Analyst,
Concurrent Technologies Corp.

"Choose your career by what it is that you enjoy doing the most."

Millions of people flow into the work world every year. Some take the job that is closest to their home, offered the fastest, appears easy to do, pays the most, or carries the most prestige. All of these are great, but nothing can substitute for really liking what you are doing. If you like doing it you will put in a great deal more effort and time, you will study to learn more, and you will perform better than everyone else who finds it a burden. It is much easier to become great at something you love than at something that does not interest you.

Beth Cummings

Training and Coaching
Consultant

*"Focus on doing what you love
and truly believe in."*

It is easy to accept any job that is offered and to do whatever you are told to do. It is much harder to hold out for a position doing what you love and staying on track with that love.

Chapter 11: Passion

Dr. Bill Swartout

Director of Technology,
USC Institute for Creative
Technologies

"Pick a job that sounds like
it will be the most interesting
and the most fun, as opposed
to the job that might make you
the most money or prestige. "

Bill believes that, "If you bet on deferred goals like wealth
or fame, there is 1) a good chance you won't achieve it and
2) even if you do, it won't be nearly as rewarding or allur-
ing once you have it. That is particularly bad if you don't
enjoy what you're doing to get there. On the other hand, if
you truly enjoy your work, you are getting your reward
as you go—and you might get fame and wealth as well."

Tom Feeney

Senior Partner,
Fowler, O'Quinn, Feeney & Sneed, P.A.

"Be passionate about pursuing
your dreams and goals. Do
what you love and love what
you do. In America there are no
limits on success."

In addition to a passion for what you do, Tom emphasizes
the unlimited opportunities that are available in America.

Buck Leahy

Owner,
Buck Leahy Consulting &
Communications, LLC

"Do what you love, and keep your promises—there will be no limits for you!"

There are a few big regulators on how far you can go and Buck identifies two of them. You have to keep your promises if other people are going to trust you enough to keep doing business with you. You have to do what you really love if you are going to generate enough energy, enthusiasm, and effort to keep doing it well for many years.

Nephi Lewis

Product Manager,
Rockwell Collins Simulation
and Training Solutions

"The secret of life is not to do what you like, but to like what you do."—American Proverb.

There are fascinating and rewarding aspects of almost every job. If you are tired to doing a job, you need to find these positive aspects. If you cannot change jobs, you can still change your attitude about the job you have.

Chapter 11: Passion

Norman Chait

Director,
Merrill Lynch

"Be passionate about what you do."

You did not accept this job so you could sit back and be bad at it. Jump in and do your very best. Impress the company with how hard you work and make them glad they chose you.

Priscilla Elfrey

Simulation Liaison,
NASA Kennedy Space Center

"People get paid to do more things than you can possibly imagine, so concentrate on something that drives your passion."

How many different jobs are there in the world? The number is almost uncountable. If you can imagine it, then someone is probably making a living doing it. If that is what you are passionate for then go looking for it - it probably exists out there somewhere.

Thomas Casill

President,
MacGregor Abstract Company

"Find something that you love
to do and you will never have
to work!"

What is the difference between work, hobbies, and play? Generally it is just the degree to which you are internally motivated to do each of them. If you can find a job you love to do, then who says it should be called work? Some people get paid to do what they love. Others get paid to do what they hate. Which do you want to be?

Dr. Richard Fujimoto

Division Chair,
Georgia Institute of Technology

"Figure out what you are passionate about, what gets you out of bed in the morning."

Richard says, "This is what you will be good at. Then, find a job where you can do this, every day."

Chapter 11: Passion

Michael McCoy

Professor of Design,
Southern Methodist University

"Working for a paycheck in a
job you hate usually ends in
disaster."

Do what you love, be passionate about it, and all else in life
will follow.

Leaders share their most valued words of guidance

Hamilton Hitchings

Director,
Linden Labs

"Follow your passion."

The popular Second Life world was created by people who
had a vision and a passion for a new kind of software - a
virtual world that was not a game, but an alternate place to
live and interact with other people.

Michael Clark

*Principle Consultant,
Heritage Consulting*

"Make sure you do nothing just for the money."

We do so many things based on our personal passion. But when it comes to our jobs and careers, we fall into the trap of measuring everything in dollars. Treat your career like other areas that interest you—follow your passion, not the money.

Chapter 12

PERSISTENCE

Steve Painter

Division Manager,
Cobham Analytic Solutions

"In the words of Winston Churchill... 'Never, never give up!'"

Winston Churchill's statements were simple and so powerful that we still echo them sixty years later. England could have chosen to surrender during the darkest days of World War II when they stood almost alone against Hitler's forces. But they resolved to never give up.

Noah Falstein

Freelance Game Designer,
The Inspiracy

"Talent, skill, and experience
are important, but ultimately
persistence seems to trump
them all when it comes to
getting a good start."

You will face thousands of little problems and challenges in
your work. Some of these require brilliance to solve. Some
require a team effort. But most of them require buckling
down and just working hard to get through them. Do you
have the persistence to tackle and solve one tough problem
after another? Can you get excited by seeing yourself overcome a string of these challenges?

John Walker

Founding Director,
Navigant Consulting

"Never give up—even when the odds are against you—you just never know how things are going to work out."

Every action, every relationship, every challenge contains within it the seeds of greater opportunity. If you give up you do not get to find and exploit these seeds. Your own ability to see into the future is terrible. You can only see what is happening right now and have faith that working hard now will lead to better opportunities in the future. Quitting never leads to better opportunities.

Nephi Lewis

Product Manager,
Rockwell Collins Simulation and
Training Solutions

"The characteristic of heroism
is its persistency."

"All men have wandering impulses, fits and starts of generosity. But when you have chosen your part, abide by it, and do not weakly try to reconcile yourself with the world. The heroic cannot be the common, nor the common heroic. Yet we have the weakness to expect the sympathy of people in those actions whose excellence is that they outrun sympathy and appeal to a tardy justice. If you would serve your brother because it is fit for you to serve him, do not take back your words when you find that prudent people do not commend you."—Ralph Waldo Emerson

Kim Hahn

CEO,
Intellectual Capital Productions

"Do it again. Life is like a menu and you should sample many choices."

Kim has held a number of positions and knows that you do not necessarily stumble into your ideal situation with your first job—or the second—or the third. Just keep looking, the world is an incredibly diverse and rich place. You have just scratched the surface of all of the possibilities.

Dannie Cutts

Senior Computer Scientist,
Aegis Technologies Group

"Remain patient and resilient."

"Your career may take many turns that you don't understand, but those twists and turns and valleys can make
you a better person."

Catherine Wyman

Program Director,
DeVry University

"Don't quit."

There are thousands of people who know how to give up
when the job gets difficult. There are very few who steel
themselves to keep going and discover an inner strength
that they did not know they had.

Chapter 12: Persistence

Gabriel Ruiz

Army Program Field Executive,
CDW-G

"Don't take 'no' for an answer,
even from your boss, when
your heart tells you otherwise."

"No" means that someone else does not want your idea to
happen. It does not mean that your idea, your ambition,
your dream is wrong or bad. It means that the other person
does not want it for themselves. If your heart tells you that
something is important to you, then you have to pursue it.

Nephi Lewis

Product Manager,
Rockwell Collins Simulation
and Training Solutions

"Advantage comes not from the spectacular or the technical. Advantage comes from a persistent seeking of the mundane edge." —Tom Peters

Can you be just a little better than those around you? Can you make just one more sale, get one more answer right, fix just one more problem? It is the smallest edges that make the difference between those who win and those who place second. In an Olympic race the difference between a gold medal and 4th place can be less than one second.

Chapter 12: Persistence

Joseph Tranfo

Managing Principal,
Benedict Capital, LLC

"80% of success is showing up."

If 80% of success is showing up, that means that only 20% of the people are doing it. Most people don't know that showing up is the necessary prerequisite to getting anything done. They think the world will wait for them if they are late. It won't. The world will just leave without you.

Noah Falstein

Freelance Game Designer,
The Inspiracy

"Be politely persistent."

Noah has designed some of the best computer games on the planet, many of them classics. He started when gaming was a backroom, niche market and big business did not believe in it. Under those conditions, persistence will take you farther than talent, skill, and experience. You just have to keep on plugging at it because you believe in what you are doing.

Chapter 13

PLANNING

Trent Tuggle

Senior Engineer,
SPARTA Inc.

"Never be fooled into thinking that you are the summation of your resume."

Your greatest strengths will probably never be discussed in your resume. The day that you find your yourself adequately captured in your resume may be the day that you should become concerned for your future.

Chapter 13: Planning

Damon Regan

*Solutions Engineer,
Eduworks Corporation*

"People, Purpose, and Place—
you're in the right spot when
the 3P's align."

Are you working with the right people? Do you have a purpose in your work? Are you in the place that you need to be to be effective? If you can get all three of these to align, then you are going to be happy, valuable, and effective in your work.

Dave Edstrom

Chief Technologist—
Global Systems Engineering,
Sun Microsystems

"Always pay yourself first."

You work to earn all of the money that is in your paycheck. But you give all of it to other people and companies. How much do you keep for yourself and your future? Paying yourself first means taking a set amount from your check every month and putting it in savings and investments. It means treating your future as if it is more important than the profits and products at every retailer in town.

Abraham Lloyd

Senior Consultant,
Twin Technologies

"A goal without a plan is
nothing more than a wish."

Make a plan on how to reach your goals. This is the same as climbing a mountain. It may be clear where you want to go. But you have to plan a path to get there.

Adam Martinez

Management Consultant,
Washington DC

"In accounting terms, don't let the sunk costs sink you."

Sunk costs are those that you have already put into a project. You cannot get these back out again. Just because you have invested a lot of money and time in a project does not mean you have to keep on investing in it. You can stop. You can say—this is not working and it is never going to work. You do not have to let the sunk costs keep on sinking you.

Audrey Spolarich

Health Consultant,
Washington DC

"Put a date on everything."

When will you finish a project? When will you learn a new skill? When will you deliver a product? Put a date on everything you really want to accomplish. Do not let important things drift into the "some day" future. You have to nail it down so you are motivated to get on top of it and deliver on your commitments—especially when those commitments are to yourself.

David Bergerson

Vice President,
Sixpoint Partners

"Planning differentiates dream from reality."

We all know that it takes action to move from a dream to a reality. But which actions? A plan is the map that shows you which actions should be taken, in what order, how long they should take, and what results are expected. If you want to move from your current reality to the one you are dreaming of, you need a plan.

Chapter 13: Planning

Mike O'Dell

Chief Scientist,
UUNET

"Scaling is always the problem."

Mike developed some of the earliest software that makes up the Internet. All software begins as a single line of code and then grows bigger. It is impossible to see how big a software project can get, but eventually you have turned a very small program into a very large system. Creating something that can scale from its small beginnings to the Internet that connects the entire world is a huge challenge.

Leaders share their most valued words of guidance

Dr. Joe LaViola

Assistant Professor,
University of Central Florida

"It's okay to fail. Failure breeds
success."

You will come to appreciate that you learn a great deal from
your failures and much less from your successes. All failure
is temporary and just gives you an opportunity to become
stronger so you can succeed in the future.

Will Calloway

Account Executive,
Apple Computer

"Don't feel like you have to define your career right after college. Most people work several jobs before they truly figure out what they want to do."

College does not prepare you for the end of your life, it prepares you for the beginning. Take it as a good starting point, but not a good ending point. You have a great deal of terrain to cover in your life and you will be significantly different at the end than you are at the beginning.

Adam Martinez

Management Consultant,
Washington DC

"It is never to late to make a good decision."

Adam believes that, "Sometimes you make a good decision that turns out badly and you feel stuck with the results. But if at a later time you recognize that another decision is the right one for the new now, then change to it."

Dr. MB Sarkar

Professor of Business,
Temple University

"Create and pursue
opportunities."

MB believes that, "Whether it is to improve the bottom line
or to create new markets for your organization, or in your
dealings with other individuals—seek to create new value
and then pursue this aggressively. To do this you need a
holistic set of skills ranging from an acute awareness of
the new globality, to sensitivity in dealing with individuals."

Don Philpitt

Deputy Director,
Joint Coalition Simulation
Systems

"Think before you act."

Think before you react. Think before you speak. Be in control of your responses to people and situations. Don't let your emotional reactions overcome your better judgment.

Chapter 14

PRACTICAL

Dr. Stacy Trammell

Owner,
Zavda Technologies Inc.

"Put your services and small business attributes on the back of your business cards."

Stacy says, "This has led to new business opportunities for me and serves as a wonderful billboard. Also, as a new business owner I say patience and persistence are essential. It took me one to two years to develop the business connections that I depend on today."

Donna Day

Liaison,
US Department of Defense

"Get it in writing…"

"He said this and she said that", are a terrible way to document an agreement or a situation. Write it down, capture it in email, put it in a document. This is a big help toward insuring that everyone is on the same sheet of music.

Ray Giroux

Senior Software Engineer,
Forterra Inc.

"Keep a professional notebook."

"If your company does not already provide some kind of notebook, go buy a composition notebook. Keep notes on the events of the day, take notes at meetings even if the meeting is just one on one, jot down important blurbs and data. By taking notes and keeping these organized you can reference information weeks or months later."

Bryan Cole

President,
Cole Engineering Service Inc.

"Build systems that are easy
for customers to use."

Bryan is thinking of his customers for defense products.
He wants to see these from the point of view of the soldiers
who have to use them. They may work for the engineers
making them, but do they work for the soldiers? Do these
systems solve the problem that the customer has?

Mike Friedman

Advanced Concepts Analyst,
Concurrent Technologies Corp.

"Don't attempt to create proprietary solutions, but try to create learning solutions which can interoperate with existing standards."

Your customers need solutions that they can fit into their businesses. They do not need to be limited by the shape and capability of your products. Give them the flexibility to achieve their goals and they will reward you with the business you are eager to receive.

Chapter 14: Practical

Barbara McDaniel

Director, Conferences and Programs,
National Training and Simulation Association

"Tuck in your shirt."

What do you look like to the world? You are being judged by your appearance. That is why your mother always told you to tuck in your shirt and stand up straight.

Ronda Henning

Senior Scientist,
Harris Corporation

"Never eat a powdered sugar donut in a dark suit."

You have seen these donuts at meetings. Who thought that was a good idea? You can eat these at home. But when you are wearing a dark suit go for the plain or chocolate donuts.

John Tufarolo

Sr. Principal Engineer,
Raytheon Inc.

"Make meetings interactive—
not presentations. Don't be
afraid of asking questions."

John believes that, "Too many times meetings are held where one person does all the talking and the rest sit, listen, then leave. The incorrect assumption is that everyone has the same understanding. If you take the initiative to ask questions, many misconceptions or misunderstandings can be uncovered early or avoided altogether."

Dr. Dean Hartley

Hartley Consulting

"Learn to touch type and take a course in accounting."

You are going to spend hours working at a computer You had better be able to fly through that keyboard because it will directly influence how much work you can get done.

Jay Roland

President,
Roland & Associates

"Any advice that would fit on the back of a business card and be legible is probably not worth reading."

Roland is a man of deep thoughts and experiences. He believes in telling his story in many words, examples, and data. His guidance will not fit on the back of a business card.

Chapter 15

RELATIONSHIPS

Dave Edstrom

Chief Technologist—
Global Systems Engineering,
Sun Microsystems

"Never, ever, sleep with someone who has more problems than you do."

If you think you have a lot of your own problems, you just try getting into a tight relationship with someone who has more problem than you do. You are going to find out how well you can carry your own problems and those of another person.

Dr. Tom Mastaglio

President,
MYMIC, LLC

"As in school, in business there are 3 "R's" which are the keys to success: relationships, results and reputation! "

Tom has served in the US Army, been a leader in large companies, and started his own small business. Through all of this he can identify relationships, results, and reputation as the three most important things in your career. You need relationships to accomplish big things. Success means delivering results to build your reputation. Your reputation will determine whether people will work with you.

Dr. David Pratt

CTO and Fellow,
SAIC

"Your value to the organization is measured in the boss' eyes, not your own."

Do you have the objectivity and humility to see your work from your boss' perspective? To do this you have to know what is important to your boss and what he thinks your contributions should be. This may be very different from what you think you are contributing.

Dr. Aubrey Lee

Management Consultant,
SESCO

"If you don't want it done to you don't do it."

Aubrey believes that the Golden Rule works in both directions. Do not do unto others what do not want them to do unto you.

Dr. Jeff Wilkinson

Chief Scientist & CTO,
MYMIC

"Who else needs to know? Information is power only when you share it."

The old practice of keeping information secret as a means to power is out. Today, all information is available from multiple sources. Your power comes from being a current and reliable source of information. Find ways to share information as fast as possible. This will create real power across the entire organization.

Chapter 15: Relationships

Gabriel Ruiz

Army Program Field Executive,
CDW-G

"Do and ask for favors, this
empowers you and exalts
others."

Gabe recognizes that people really enjoy helping others.
When you ask someone for a favor you give them the opportunity to show how effective they can be. You are asking
them to show their talents and their humanity. Doing a
favor for another person is an opportunity to show how
much you care about other people.

Dr. Sudhir Srinivasan

Technical Director,
NetApp Inc.

"Choose your boss carefully."

Your progress in a company is going to be directly tied to
your boss—what he thinks about you, how he uses you,
and what he thinks should become of you and your career.
If you tie yourself to someone who just wants to take what
you have to offer and give back as little as possible you are
going to be in a losing situation. Be very careful in deciding
who you are willing to work for. It will make a big difference
in where your career goes.

Dr. Thom McLean

Principle Engineering Manager,
Rockwell Collins

"Treat everyone you meet as
if they will end up being your
boss."

"This has served me very well when heeded and burned
me when not. It is dangerously easy to hastily assess a
person's importance in one's life or career when first meeting them. We tend to size up the importance of a person
by their achievements, their position, title, influence, and
wealth. It is tempting, as one starts out, to draw a bright
line between those we consider peers and those we think of
as our seniors. As we mature in our career, it is equally
tempting to brand people as juniors, permitting ourselves
to be dismissive or insular in dealing with those who have
not yet 'paid their dues' or don't 'have stature' in the field."

Doug Roberts

Business Development,
EDS

"Always treat the customer as you would want to be treated. When supporting the customer its better to ask for forgiveness after going too far, than for permission before acting at all."

Doug is echoing the Golden Rule in the first part of his advice—do unto others as you would have them do unto you. In the second part, he advises that supporting the customer is so important that you should go overboard in doing the right thing. If you go too far, it is much better to ask your boss' forgiveness for helping the customer too much.

Eric Preisz

Business Developer,
Garage Games

"You don't earn respect with what or how much you know. You earn it by enabling others to get more things done more easily."

Eric works in the computer game business which attract some very smart people. But smart is not enough to earn respect. Your presence, your efforts, and your intelligence need to make a contribution to the work of others if you want their respect.

Kimberly Love

Project Manager,
University of Pittsburg Medical Center

"Understand the importance of networking within your own company."

"While we see numerous articles emphasizing the importance of networking within an industry or city, younger people don't always network within their own company. I was one of those people. Now, I understand the importance of these contacts towards success in my current position as well as in terms of a promotion or a move within the company. You may not have to leave a company to get the position you really want if you have a strong internal network."

Chapter 15: Relationships

Bob Neches

Director of the Distributed Scalable
Systems Division,
Information Sciences Institute,
University of Southern California

"Never use your own words to
convince someone when their
words will do."

Bob believes that, "it's easier to persuade people if you
make the effort to understand their thinking, rather than
expecting them to understand yours"

Patrick Crane

VP of Marketing,
LinkedIn

"Consider the potential of every relationship you develop. How can you help this person? How can this person help you?"

Relationships create a supportive social fabric. They allow individuals to draw upon the strengths of others. This is one of the major factors that have made humans so prosperous on the planet.

Dr. Doug Reece

Research Scientist,
Applied Research Associates

"Be positive and constructive
in your dealings with people."

Doug says, "Don't dismiss, criticize or insult people, ideas,
or organizations because you first don't agree with them
or judge them to be bad. Listen and consider. You may
learn they have merit that you didn't know about. Negative comments can hurt you if you interact with these
people again in the future."

Dr. Curt Blais

Research Fellow,
Naval Postgraduate School

"Make your workplace a fun place to be for you and your fellow workers."

We all spend a great deal of time in our offices, with our coworkers, and involved in our projects. Make a contribution to the fun and enjoyable atmosphere that surrounds all of this. There is no reason that work has to be miserable.

Albert Johnson

Member, Board of Directors,
Industrial Research Institute

"The most important thing
you must do in business is to
sincerely say, 'Thank You'."

We all benefit from the help, support, and contributions of
other people. But most of us never say thank you for those
contributions.

Dr. Aubrey Lee

Management Consultant,
SESCO

*"Business deals fail.
Relationships endure."*

Though one deal might fail, you are likely to find yourself doing another deal with some of the same people. Do not cut yourself off from people just because the last deal did not work out.

Ben Ross

Account Executive for IT Practice,
Forrest Solutions

"The rainmaker always treats everyone with respect—you never know how people are connected."

Many ancient cultures contain a story about a rich and powerful man who appeared common and ordinary. Then when someone was kind to him, he rewarded them with riches or power. These are admonishions to respect all men.

Danny Thomas

Senior Research Scientist,
Aegis Technologies Group

"We solved most of the problems that one person can do a long time ago. Modeling space flight or missile defense is too complex for one person to tackle alone."

For any significant problem you will be working with a team of people. The solo problems in engineering are largely a thing of the past. In fact, as we move forward, very diverse and multi-disciplinary teams are going to become more common because we are running out of problems that can be solved by a team of people who all have the same skills.

Eric Root

Program Manager,
SAIC

"Be helpful when someone asks
for assistance or information,
and treat everyone with
respect."

Many industrial communities is really very small. The professionals in them work with and interact with the same group of people for years. The first impression you leave with someone could be with you for a long time.

John Hathaway

Software Architect,
Dow Jones

"Work on personal politics and communication skills, they are as important as technical skills."

Working with other people in a diplomatic manner is as important as being able to build a rocket or program a computer.

Jon Watte

CTO,
Forterra Systems

"Make and maintain friends
outside of your field of
expertise."

Be involved in multiple social circles. The world is a rich and
diverse place. You probably have not found your best home
in it yet. Diverse friends will introduce you to new parts of
this world.

Karen Parker

*Senior Manager,
Lockheed Martin*

"Help others."

Your work here on Earth is not just to support yourself. You are making a contribution to the lives of many other people. Work for the good of others—that is the real measure of the value of your life.

Dr. Mike Macedonia

Vice President and General Manager,
Forterra Federal Systems

"Your greatest source of satisfaction will not come from the work, but from the people you work with."

Mike explains, "My father, a psychologist, once told me that people hire others who look like them. Its true. What he was telling me was that companies and organizations are made of people and their basic instincts will seep into every task, including hiring. You will look like your boss and your future boss will look like you. Your greatest source of satisfaction will not come from the work, but the people you work with."

Dr. Ricardo Valerdi

Research Associate,
MIT

"The technical problems are easier than the people problems. Engineering is a team sport."

Even the nerds in engineering need people skills and networks to achieve their goals.

Roger Goff

HPC Architect and Principle Engineer,
Sun Microsystems

"Building your network of contacts is the single most important thing you can do in the current workplace environment where companies are no longer loyal to their employees."

Roger says, "75% of all new jobs are found through your network of contacts. More career opportunities will come your way because of the people who know what you can do."

Shaun Schneider

Account Manager,
TEKsystems

"Develop great relationships and know who your champions are."

Within your network of friends, peers, and professional associates there are a few people who are champions for you. Do you know who these people are? Do you appreciate them and make the most of the leverage they give you in the world?

Steve Hinksman

Program Manager,
A-T Solutions

"Deliver what you promised,
and if what you promised
isn't what was expected, talk
it out—maybe you can meet
halfway."

Steve knows that, "Meeting customer expectations is sometimes difficult, especially when what was negotiated isn't really what they want or need. This is true for internal customers, like supervisors and other departments, and the traditional external customers and end-users. The immediate effect on your career path may not be obvious, but a long-term reputation for respect and honesty opens a lot of doors."

Chapter 16

FAMOUS

Charles Darwin

Scientist

"It is not the strongest of the species that survive, nor the most intelligent, but the one most responsive to change."

Charles Darwin's entire theory of species is based on the importance of adaptation and change. Strength and intelligence are not valuable if they can not be adapted to the current situation. The people and the species who have the ability to change themselves in order to handle a changing world are the ones who will be the most successful.

Ghandi

Indian Political Leader

"You must be the change you wish to see in the world."

Ghandi saw the injustice in India and made himself the change agent for the problem. He believed in personal responsibility and personal action to make the world a better place.

Walt Disney

Founder,
Walt Disney Company

"Do what you do so well that they will want to see it again and bring their friends."

Walt Disney created a fantasy world like no one had ever seen. He knew that the secret to making it a worldwide success was to make it so good that people would come again and again. He believed in excellence at a level that would impress the entire world.

Seneca

Roman Poet

"As is a tale, so is life: not how long it is, but how good it is, is what matters."

Would you enjoy a long, dull book, with no inspiring insight, and no beloved characters? Or a story of excitement lived, dreams pursued, people in love, a world changed, and meaningful words of guidance? Your life is just such a tale. How will you write it?

George Washington

President of the United States

"Good moral character is the first essential in a man."

George Washington became famous for his integrity. He led the country as a soldier, a politician, a land owner, and a citizen. From all of these perspectives he saw the importance of moral character.

Chapter 16: Famous

Aristotle

Philosopher

"The educated differ from the uneducated as much as the living from the dead."

Even 2,300 years ago Aristotle could see the fundamental impact that education has on people and a population. He knew that the progress of humankind was more dependent upon education than hard work. Working hard at the same things you did yesterday will keep the organization running just like it ran yesterday. But moving forward requires learning, education, and new knowledge.

Leaders share their most valued words of guidance

Dio Chrysostom

Philosopher

"Why oh why are human beings so hard to teach, but so easy to deceive?"

Millions of people are deceived into believing there is an easy path to success, riches, and happiness. If only they absorbed new knowledge as easily as they were misled, the world would be a much more advanced place.

Confucius

Philosopher

"I hear and I forget
I see and I remember
I do and I understand."

Action and experience are much more effective teachers than listening and watching. Get involved. Don't be afraid to stumble and make mistakes. You will understand more than everyone who is just learning with their ears and eyes.

Woody Allen

Actor & Director

"Half of the secret to success in life is just showing up."

Most people are very lax in their work and their attendance. They miss days. They show up late. They leave early. You can be more successful than half of the world just by showing up consistently. Just by being there to do something.

J K Rowling

Author, Harry Potter Series

"Failure gave me an inner security that I had never attained by passing examinations."

This author learned through her failures that she had a strong will and a great deal of discipline. These traits were not brought out through traditional school work and would have remained hidden from her if not for the failures that demanded that she use them.

Dwight Eisenhower

President of the United States

"In preparing for battle I have always found that plans are useless but planning is indispensible."

General Eisenhower was in charge of all Allied Forces in Europe during World War II. He planned the invasions of France and Germany. But this great planner felt that the plans themselves were useless because war and business are such complex and dynamic endeavors that the situations you plan for change as soon as you begin executing the plan. But the act of planning is indispensible because it builds in your mind an understanding of all of the players and possible events that can occur.

Chapter 16: Famous

Ghandi

Indian Political Leader

"A man is but the product of his thoughts. What he thinks, he becomes."

Your thoughts guide your actions, or inactions. Your actions are your life and your person. What you think controls who you become.

Brian Tracy

Business Consultant

"Work all of the time that you work."

Did you know that most of the people in your organization do not work there? They come in late. They waste time around the water cooler. They sit idle while waiting for someone to tell them what to do. They take no initiative. They do not see themselves as a part of the success of the organization. You can outperform more than half of your peers just by working all of the time that you are at work.

Chapter 16: Famous

Scott Adams

Creator of Dilbert Cartoon

"1. Become the best at one specific thing.
2. Become very good (top 25%) at two or more things.
3. Become a good public speaker.
#1 is very rare, but most people can accomplish #2 and #3 with effort. "

Scott Adams has created an incredibly successful business. Dilbert is published, recognized, and quoted all over the world. Scott believes there are three ways to be successful. One is to be the very best in the world at one specific thing. The best basketball player or the best runner are rare. So this avenue is only open to a few people. The second is to become very good at two or more things that you can leverage together. He believes that this path is open to a great many people. And finally, he believes that you should become a good public speaker because it reveals your expertise to the world.

Anatole France

French Poet,
Nobel Prize Winner in Literature

"To accomplish great things, we must not only act, but also dream; not only plan, but also believe."

Your thoughts and your actions work together to accomplish great things. You cannot accomplish these without action. You cannot accomplish them without believing.

Marilyn Monroe

Actress

"I don't want to make money, I just want to be wonderful."

Marilyn was focused on contributing her unique persona to the world. She was not in show business for the money, but for the impact that she would have on the world that watched her.

Chapter 17

FAVORITES

Ghandi

Indian Political Leader

"A man is but the product of his thoughts. What he thinks, he becomes."

Charles Darwin

Scientist

"It is not the strongest of the species that survive, nor the most intelligent, but the one most responsive to change."

Bob Neches

Director of the Distributed Scalable Systems Division, Information Sciences Institute, University of Southern California

"Don't throw away this card."

Dr. Joe LaViola

Assistant Professor,
University of Central Florida

"It's okay to fail. Failure breeds success."

Irantzu Gonzalez

International Marketing Manager,
BMW Group

"If you are not online, you do not exist."

Jim Stogsdill

CTO, Mission Systems,
Accenture

"Follow the rules, until you're
ready not to."

LtCol. Peter Garretson

Chief,
Air Force Future Science and
Technology Exploration

"Duty is knowing what needs to be done and when it needs to be done without having to be told that it needs to be done."

Al Morasso

Director,
Educational Testing Service

"Neither the peaks, nor the valleys in your career should concern you, but rather the plateaus."

Marco Pluijm

Manager Port Development,
Amsterdam Port Authority

"If I can't be myself, who else
should I be?"

Ken Shuster

Added Value Solutions

"You cannot read the
handwriting on the wall if you
are one of the bricks."

Bill Waite

*Chairman and CTO,
Aegis Technologies Group*

"You can do anything... but not everything."

Dr. Katherine Morse

Senior Staff,
Johns Hopkins University

"Learn to write with precision and clarity. If you can't express your idea, it doesn't exist."

www.ingramcontent.com/pod-product-compliance
Lightning Source LLC
Chambersburg PA
CBHW021031210326
41598CB00016B/981